Master the Art of Swedish Death Cleaning [Döstädning]

A Charming, Practical, and Unsentimental Approach to Organize and Declutter Your Home and Life—Workbook Included

Ingrid Johansson

Table of Contents

Introduction

Is your life riddled with clutter? Do you have to go through dozens of items that you don't use each day only to pull out the one item you need? Throughout life, most collect items, like memorabilia, decorations, office supplies, and others that seem important and useful. Yet, after a while, you may find yourself looking at a shelf or a closet full of random things that you no longer recall wanting or needing. What happened? The answer lies in the fact that you likely didn't need those items as much to begin with, and over time, they lost all importance to you. Yet, you've been avoiding to clear them out for so long that you're now stuck with a whole storage worth of clutter, an unclear idea about what to do with it, and a looming sense of guilt for letting it go as you suspect that those items were meaningful at one point or another.

Your ideal decluttering solution may not be to throw it out all at once, as you might regret it later on. It may also not be in trying to keep and sort everything, as this will only result in the endless growth of clutter piles. What should you do? The answer is- try Swedish death cleaning! Wait... What? Swedish death cleaning is a perfect middle ground between practical and emotional decisions in keeping and letting go of items. It takes into account one simple question: Which belongings you want to remain behind after your passing? This may sound strange, indeed. Morbid, even. But if you look at the meaning of it, you'll realize that this way of cleaning makes you think about which of your belongings are so meaningful that you want them to remain after you? This is an important question, which makes you think about the value that your items have and how they represent you as a person, and your whole life.

Swedish death cleaning is also a practical concept. It acknowledges the need to live in the present moment, with all of the necessary items at the arm's reach, calling for some careful thinking, categorizing, and sorting, to figure out what you truly need. This is where this book comes! In your organizing and cleaning manual Master the Art of Swedish Death Cleaning [Döstädning], you will explore the principles and strategies of Swedish Death Cleaning, including:

- **Sorting and categorizing your belongings.**

Master the Art of Swedish Death Cleaning [Döstädning]: A Charming, Practical, and Unsentimental Approach to Organize and Declutter Your Home and Life - Workbook

Included will help you find out what you need, should/must keep, and what you can let go of; this will help you make better decisions when it comes to future shopping and deciding on which items you truly need and want, and which ones aren't necessary in the long run. Not only will you save a lot on shopping, but you'll also be able to make more meaningful and wholesome choices regarding what you bring into your home in the long run.

Being more organized and having less built-up clutter over time. Being organized is a habit, not a one-time task. Having gone through the process of managing your items from scratch will help you maintain the same "organized mindset" in the long run. Imagine knowing where each of your items should live even before you buy it, and having that ingrained in your memory without having to make a lot of conscious effort. Swedish death cleaning will help you form this useful habit so that staying organized long-term requires a lot less effort!

- **Have a deeper understanding of your belongings and make better decisions in the future.**

The kind of wholesome relationship with your items that's promoted in this book will help you look at everything you buy through the lens of its value, significance, and practical use for you and your household. You will not suffer regret for overspending and impulse shopping as you realize that the luxury item that you just got doesn't serve any purpose. You will learn to choose those items that will have both practical and emotional meaning, which will make them more useful and enjoyable.

- **Create a more organized and clutter-free home.**

Having a home that's easier to keep clean and orderly will help you minimize stress and anxiety long-term. It could also make your household cheaper to clean and maintain if you're paying for cleaning, or even make it as simple to go over once a week as for you to decide that you can now afford to have someone clean for you, in case you weren't doing that before. Or, if you do your own cleaning, organizing it well can make cleaning and tidying as practical as being able to deep-clean an entire house in less than a few hours!

- **How to organize your sentimental items and memorabilia.**

Some of our things aren't practical and useful at all; they might have pure sentimental value, or be a bit more valuable in material terms. Whichever it is, you need to find a way to organize them in a way that makes their actual value to you and your family shine through. It might be a set of silver cutlery or your child's clay sculpture from when they were six years old. If an item carries significance for you, it should be kept. However, it is also important to know how to store and display your items. Your kids' little clay sculpture needs to be protected and preserved, whereas the silver cutlery needs to be carefully polished, and set in a box or a canteen, where you can easily pull it out and clean it when needed. You will learn how to do all that in this book, plus some more! You will learn how to preserve your personal history and let the items that depict who you are as a person, your lineage, and what means most to you in life remain as a legacy for your loved ones. You will also connect with your past by honoring the memories of friends and family members who have passed away. Altogether, this will provide you with a greater sense of self-awareness and personal fulfillment. Swedish Death Cleaning has something to offer to everyone. Start your journey TODAY, and begin moving towards a more organized and fulfilling life!

Chapter 1: Getting Started With Swedish Death Cleaning

Understanding the Concept of Swedish Death Cleaning

Now, you're likely taken aback by the use of the word "death" right from the get-go in this manual, and for so many times. Before you even proceed reading further, let's first reframe its meaning. In the context of purging and decluttering, the idea of death here means to strip away the meaningless, materialistic, superficial, and unnecessary influences on ourselves and our lives that cause so much stress and anxiety in our daily lives. Granted, some of these things are needed and should be stored in some way, like your medical history and other relevant paperwork, spare linens, or tools. These things we may not use daily, and we may not think of them as necessary. Yet, on a few occasions in our lives when they do become necessary, not having them by your side can cause serious trouble. In that sense, the context of death here is broader than just the end of life. It also refers to the death of wasting your time and energy on mundane tasks that are eating up your time to create a living space for yourself that's meaningful, purposeful, and functional. An example of "death cleaning" that you might have done, but haven't noticed, would be the type of selection, purging, and organization that you do when moving into another home. Since many people (literally) can't afford to move all of their possessions from one place to another, they only take those items with them that are essential and have actual value and meaning. With this in mind, there's a chance that you did a bit of death cleaning long before you learned about this concept in the form you're seeing now.

To sum up, Swedish Death Cleaning is the act of decluttering and reorganizing your possessions with your mind set on leaving behind a meaningful legacy. This form of cleaning entails that you go through your belongings and decide what you want to keep, what you wish to donate, and what is completely unnecessary and should be thrown out.

Origins of Swedish Death Cleaning

Now, the term used here is anything but a marketing strategy or a tagline that aims to be memorable and ingrain itself into your mind. Swedish Death cleaning is a cultural tradition that originated in Sweden. It has been practiced for centuries by people who wanted to simplify their lives by reducing the number of their belongings and keeping only those of the highest value for them. That way, they reduce the burden on their loved ones after they pass away. Over time, people further developed this concept and embraced it as something that can be done whether or not you're preparing yourself for this life stage. As it turned out, this form of cleaning could be done as often as a person needed it, and it had numerous other benefits to one's life and well-being.

Benefits of Swedish Death Cleaning

Here are some of the major benefits of choosing Swedish death cleaning:

- **Reducing anxiety.** Swedish Death Cleaning may help ease stress and anxiousness for you and your loved ones whether or not you're preparing for passing on. On the one hand, doing that part of the work while you're still there and present can help you and your family members better understand which of your possessions are truly important and meaningful, and it also helps them in the sense of having to do less work surrounding your belongings in the event of your passing. If this isn't your main motivation for purging and reorganizing, just the fact that your whole family gets to enjoy life without clutter and having to constantly tidy up can help instill more calmness into your living space.
- **Letting go and finding closure.** Finally, there is a psychological element to letting go of emotional burden by processing negative feelings associated with certain items, or finding closure on certain events and people by letting go of items that no longer have the same, positive meaning.

- **Feel empowered and in control.** Swedish Death Cleaning can also help you feel more in control of your life and possessions. There is a certain sense of confinement, powerlessness, and chaos associated with living in a cluttered space. You might start to feel like the sheer amount of items is wearing you down, and that a large chunk of your time must go into tidying up every day just to keep your home comfortable and presentable. Getting rid of unnecessary items, particularly those items that have a negative emotional effect on you can feel very empowering and liberating.

How Is Swedish Death Cleaning Different Compared to Traditional Decluttering?

Although Swedish Death Cleaning has many similarities with regular purging and decluttering, it is not entirely the same. At its very core, Swedish Death Cleaning is a process that revolves around preparing for the end of life. In that sense, you have a different mindset, with a completely different timeline in mind while cleaning. On the contrary, traditional decluttering is often done for convenience or organizational purposes. There are even some interior design undertones to it, with an entire industry being developed around making and using stylish organizers and practical solutions for various intents and purposes.

Additionally, Swedish Death Cleaning entails that you make decisions about sentimental items. With regular cleaning and organizing, there are some criteria by which one decides whether to keep or let go of items. However, with this form of cleaning, the emphasis is more on the emotions that you associate with personal items and heirlooms. Traditional decluttering may compel you to think about what kind of emotion an item invokes and make a decision based on that. Swedish death cleaning expands that concept to what you want your legacy to be, which slightly changes your perspective. For example, belonging to a deceased friend or relative may invoke emotional pain, at least at the moment of consideration. You may want to let go of that item as you don't want it to make you sad. Traditional decluttering tells you to do just that-get rid of the thing that makes you unhappy. However, many people who did this found themselves regretting it over time. They discovered that, after some time had passed, they began missing items that now had a different emotional meaning. If, before, an item evoked sadness because it was from a friend who has let you down and you're no longer in contact, or it was from a deceased person who you were still mourning, they might have healed after a while. They might have found closure, or events took place that changed their perception, and now they regret getting rid of those mementos. Sadly, once those items were gone, it was impossible to get them back. Swedish death cleaning inspires you to think of your items as those that will be telling a story of your life after you're gone. Both good and bad are a part of life, so, even though you might not have pleasant feelings associated with some items, you might not want to take them away from your family.

Determining Your Motivation and Goals

Swedish death cleaning focuses highly on meaning, which makes it more than necessary to go into this venture with a clear idea about what you want to achieve. In that sense, it is wise to review the reasons why you feel interested in Swedish Death cleaning, and exactly what you're trying to achieve.

Why Start Swedish Death Cleaning? There are many reasons why you might choose this form of purging. Perhaps, you want to simplify your life and have fewer belongings to tend to on a day-to-day basis. You might want to reduce clutter and make weekly and monthly cleaning easier. Some people see this kind of purging as a form of preparing for the future. It is a good way to face your mortality and come to terms with the idea of death.

Goals for Swedish Death Cleaning. Common goals with this type of purging include:

- Reducing the number of possessions you have, which makes life easier for both yourself and your family.
- Organizing your belongings, which helps not only balance out the ambiance in your home and introduce more harmony, but also helps find the items you need quickly, and
- To make it easier for your loved ones to handle your belongings after you pass away.

Measuring Success

Swedish death cleaning entails a substantial amount of time and effort. Yet, you may find yourself unsure about whether or not you're doing it correctly. Here's how you can measure your success with Swedish Death Cleaning:

- **The amount of clutter you've eliminated.** Many people find it satisfying to take pictures of boxes and bags of items that they have thrown out, as well as the image of their space before and after.
- **The number of items you've donated or thrown out.** You can also track how many items you've donated and to whom.
- **How better organized your home is.** Taking before and after photos and taking notes of how easier it is to go about your daily activities in a better-organized home is also a great way to track your success.

Benefits of Achieving Your Goals

Achieving what you've set your mind to do with Swedish death cleaning can help you reduce stress and anxiety. It can help you feel more at ease in your home environment, and improve your sleep quality. Swedish Death Cleaning can also help you improve quality of life. Minimizing your belongings will help spend less time cleaning, and more time doing things you love. Plus, beginning more meaningful items to the forefront also helps feel better emotionally, as you're surrounded by items that make you feel good. Finally, this form of purging can make it easier for your family to take care of your belongings after your passing.

Why It's Important to Set Realistic Expectations

If you ever went down the rabbit hole of looking at Pinterest for inspiration, then you know how unrealistic organization aspirations can be. People go as far as color-coding their fruits and vegetables in the refrigerator, and even photoshop their photos to make them more appealing. As a result, you might feel overly critical of yourself and think that you're not working hard enough on planning and organizing your space. The idealized expectations set by social media can make you feel like, no matter what you do, you always have too many items. It's important to set realistic expectations before you even begin organizing to avoid feeling anxious and worrying about whether or not you're doing it correctly.

Accept and Work Around Limitations

Consider the following limitations that might hinder your efforts to plan and organize your space:

- **Physical limitations**, like health conditions, strength and focus problems, as well as any mobility issues that you might have.
- **Emotional limitations**, like having difficulty parting with sentimental items, or having to go through items that might be triggering difficult feelings.
- **Time Management:** Be realistic about how much time you can commit to the process, and break it down into manageable chunks. Consider setting a schedule or timeline to help keep you on track.
- **Budget:** Consider any costs associated with Swedish Death Cleaning, such as storage containers or professional organizers. Be realistic about what you can afford and prioritize your spending accordingly.
- **Physical Limitations:** Consider enlisting the help of friends or family members, or hiring a professional organizer if necessary.
- **Overcoming Emotional Attachments:** We may attach sentimental value to items because of the memories associated with them, or because they represent a part of our identity. We may also attach value to items because of their perceived usefulness or rarity. Take time to reflect on why certain items are important to you. Consider the memories

associated with the item, and whether those memories are tied to the item itself or to the person or event it represents. Take photos of sentimental items to preserve the memories associated with them. Consider passing down sentimental items to family members or friends who will appreciate them. You can also consider donating items to charity or sell them to someone who will use and appreciate them.

Coping With the Loss of Sentimental Items

Allow yourself to grieve the loss of items that you used to love but decided that no longer have a place in your life. Acknowledge your feelings, but also be aware of the reasons why you decided to let go of the said items. It might also be helpful to focus on the positive aspects of decluttering. Think more about the benefits to your mental and physical health, and the reduced burden on your loved ones.

Chapter 2: Preparing for Swedish Death Cleaning

Being well-prepared before you start with the process of Swedish Death Cleaning helps you ease the tension of the process itself. It makes you feel in control and like you're going into the cleaning strong, with few fears and insecurities. If the number of things to sort and get rid of seems intimidating now, while it's still sitting on shelves and inside the closets, imagine what it will feel like once you pull all of it out for sorting. Many people give up on purging and organizing for that simple reason: it just looks like too much work! You can prevent feeling overwhelmed by the scope of your task with a simple act of good preparation. Planning the process from start to finish, having a general idea about the result that you wish to achieve, and of course, having all of your tools and supplies ready before your start will help you feel more confident and maintain your energy throughout the process.

The Importance of Starting Early

Starting with your Swedish death cleaning as early as possible is important for several major reasons:

- **It gives you confidence.** Feeling confident in your ability to carry out the process is important to not get overwhelmed by fear and insecurity. As someone who did Swedish Death Cleaning many times, and helped other people do it, I noticed that there's a sudden Oh-Oh feeling after one begins pulling out their belongings, and realizes that, if they only take a minute to figure out what to do with the item and where to sort it, the entire process will take months. This can be tricky, especially if a person begins with their purging unprepared, thinking they'll be able to go through all of their items in a week or so. Once this turns out to not be the case, people start to be afraid. They have a lot to do, to begin with, considering their other commitments like work and chores. When purging is added on top of that, it can appear impossible, and this is why many people give up. Taking the time to think through before you act also gives you time to mentally prepare and emotionally process the scope of what you're required to do.

- **Gives you time to plan out your cleaning and organizing.** Preparation helps you avoid time-squeezing and having to rush through sorting your items. For example, if you start organizing your bedroom, and then notice that you don't have enough organizers (or any at all), you may have to pause, go shopping, and then resume at a later date when you have the time again. This can be very disruptive to your routine, and make you frustrated with the process that should otherwise be mentally relaxing. Having everything you need to be prepared ahead before you start helps the process run smoothly and without unnecessary delays.

- **Helps avoid mental overwhelm.** After a while of cleaning, you might start to feel overwhelmed. You may lose track of what you're trying to achieve with a certain area of your home, and you may lose sight of the emotional significance that some of the items have for you and your family.

Starting to plan and prepare for your Swedish Death cleaning early gives you enough time to plan and evaluate the entire process. It's advisable to start answering more general questions, like how you want your items to be sorted, how many of your items would you want to let go of, which stages you want to involve, which people you want to include, and of course, what you want your home to look like once you're done with Swedish Death Cleaning.

Planning and preparing your things makes it easier for you to make decisions about what to keep, throw out, or donate. If you do this in a time crunch, you might end up getting rid of more things than you'd like. If you don't have enough time to reflect on what each item means to you, you might let the pressure get the best of you and get rid of the bulk of your items. Then, when the "dust has settled," you might regret some of the decisions you made. On the contrary, feeling pressured to make quick decisions might make it appealing to keep more items than you need to. After that, despite all of the effort that went into organizing, you might still experience clutter and regret keeping so many items. As you can see, neither of the extremes is a good idea. Timely and patient preparation allows you more time to organize your things. The hands-on part of the process can be exhausting physically, mentally, and emotionally. When you have enough time, you don't have to put yourself through so much strain. You can work at your own pace and ensure that you're putting items in place with the right mindset. Ultimately, taking the time to prepare yourself helps you make a plan for how you'll handle items in the future. Swedish death cleaning often isn't a one-time effort. You will likely get more items as times go by, so it would be wise for you to learn from your organizing efforts. For example, I noticed that I had a tendency of buying too many specialized items instead of multipurpose items. I ended up donating most of my specialty kitchen and household tools because I was using the multipurpose options instead. It took a while for me to realize that, and once I did, that affected my future shopping decisions.

What are some of the major benefits of starting your Swedish death cleaning preparation early?

Starting early can help ease stress and anxiety associated with having to go over all of your significant belongings and potentially deciding to give up some of them. This is an important point within itself because it involves coming to terms with the fact that some memorabilia now has a different meaning for you. For example, if a memento like a picture album or a gift from a person who has hurt you later in life makes you feel disappointed, but you've been holding on to it for a long time, the decision to do so can be excruciating. Will you decide to embrace the good memories and let go of the hurt, or you'll decide that nothing that is associated with that person should be in your life? Choosing the first requires reflecting on hurtful feelings associated with the item and choosing to forgive, while the latter requires letting go of the good memories for the sake of removing any toxic impact that the said person had on your life. Either way, it is a hard decision. When you need to make dozens or hundreds of decisions like these, paired with ongoing chores and commitments, you can't afford to think about which container to buy and how much time you have left for cleaning. It is most certainly the best to have all of those decisions made ahead of time to give you a sense of control over the things that are in your life. Having control over 'what enters your life' has a huge impact that will project itself onto your mentality and the ability to set healthy boundaries with other people, and also make it a lot easier to control the 'outside' information and events that affect you emotionally. It can also make it easier for your friends and family to handle your estate and belongings after you pass away.

Gathering the Necessary Tools and Supplies

What tools and supplies do you need? If you're purging and organizing for the first time, you may not be aware of everything that's necessary for the process. Some commonly used tools and supplies include:

- Storage containers in size and shape that match your items and surfaces,
- Labels, so that you can note which container houses which items,
- Trash bags, so that you can easily sort items, and
- Cleaning supplies. Organizing is a great opportunity for you to deep-clean your entire home. Every time you remove all items from a shelf, a cupboard, or a

draw, you can easily wipe it down. Soon enough, your entire home will feel clean and shiny inside-out. However, this will only be easy if you have all of the supplies ready.

You may also need some specialized tools and supplies, depending on the type of items that you're decluttering. This might include photo albums or specialized folders for organizing your documents and photographs.

But, where can you buy these tools and supplies? Seeing all of the organizing tools and supplies in one place can make you think that you need to find a specialty store, but you don't. In fact, the majority of the items that you'll need can be easily found in the nearest available store. The funny thing about organizers is that you're likely to see them displayed at various stores, but you rarely pay attention to them as your focus is on finding different items that you're looking for at the time. I remember seeing storage containers in my local store and thinking: "Wait, that's what these are for? Ha, I thought they are only used to freeze meals. Weird." You can find various storage containers and decorative labels at most home goods or online stores or online. You can think about what style you want them to be though, because that affects their price and may significantly impact your budget.

You can easily find cleaning supplies that can be found at a store where you normally buy them. Nothing special in that regard is needed, except for one important tip: Look for mopping kits that feature mobile cleaner holders. That way, you can keep all of your cleaning supplies, clothes, sponges, and brushes in one place and grab them quickly and easily when you need them. You can purchase more specialized tools or supplies at their designated stores. Here, I found it useful to think about the style, shape, size, and color schemes, so that your organizers are all coordinated. Doing so can add more style and harmony to your home environment.

Creating a Plan and Schedule

Before you start with your Swedish death cleaning process, it's important to map out and write down a plan. Creating a plan and schedule can help keep you on track and ensure that you're making progress toward your goals. It can also help you prioritize your time and resources, and make the most of the time you have available.

What should be included in your plan and schedule? Your plan should include a list of tasks to be completed, as well as a timeline for completing them. You may also want to include a budget and a list of resources you'll need to complete the process.

But, what's the best way to create a plan and schedule? Start by breaking down the process into manageable tasks, and estimating how long each task will take. Use a calendar or planner to schedule time for each task, and be sure to build in breaks and time for self-care. Review your plan and schedule regularly to ensure that you're making progress and staying on track.

Include Friends and Family in the Process

Why include friends and family in the process where you can fully decide on your own? including friends and family can help lessen the burden on them after you pass away, and ensure that your things are distributed according to your wishes. It can also be a way to share memories and stories associated with your possessions and include your friends and family in the process of decluttering.

Who should you include? Consider including family members, close friends, or trusted advisors who you know will respect your wishes and help you achieve your goals. You may also want to include professionals, such as estate planners or professional organizers, who can provide guidance and support.

How can you include friends and family? Start by having a conversation with your friends and family about your goals and wishes for Swedish Death Cleaning. Ask for their input and support, and be open to their suggestions and feedback. Consider including them in the process of decluttering, either by helping you sort through your things or by taking things off your hands.

There are a couple more benefits to including friends and family in your decisions. Doing so can help ensure that your things are distributed according to your wishes, and lessen the burden on your friends and family after you pass away. It can also be a way to share memories and stories associated with your things and include your friends and family in the process of decluttering.

Chapter 3: The Swedish Death Cleaning Method

Sorting and Categorizing Your Things

Once you've gone through the entire mental process of preparing and planning your organizing journey, it's time to get to work and put your plan to good use. One of the initial steps is to organize your belongings by sorting and categorizing them. Now, as transformative and refreshing as this process can be, it's also important to remember that it is highly exhausting. You go through both physical and emotional strain, so it would be wise to start only when you've had good rest and a replenishing snack. Remember to plan for regular breaks and refreshments as well! Trying to work through the bulk of the day may leave you more sensitive and irritable than you'd otherwise be. Considering that you will likely be processing plenty of intense feelings, you want to make sure that you're in the best possible headspace to do that. Now that we've cleared that out, it's time to reflect on categorizing and its importance a bit more.

Why is it important to sort and categorize your belongings?

Sorting and categorizing your items can help you identify what you have. You may have an idea of what you want your space to look like, and you might have a faint idea about the items that are most important to you. However, you may not be completely aware of all the things you have. In that sense, categorizing can make it easier to make decisions about what you want to keep, donate, or throw out. It can also help you identify patterns in the things you keep. Every person is unique, , and makes different choices when it comes to buying and keeping their things. Discovering your own patterns can make it easier to organize them in a thoughtful, more meaningful way that better reflects your behavior and personality.

How should you sort and categorize your things?

Deciding which system to use for categorization can be tricky, as there are many potential ways to choose from. You can categorize by type, use, shape, size, color, and other criteria. However, the most important thing is that the criteria are relevant when it comes to the items. For example, if you had hundreds of tools in your shed, it wouldn't make sense to first group them by color, as color is an irrelevant criterion. Instead, it would be smarter to categorize them by type first, and group certain tools together depending on how you use them and when you need them. After you've figured out the organizing criteria that you want to use, you can continue with the process.

First, group belongings together by similarity, like clothing, books, kitchenware, or another dedicated criterion that you chose. Then, you can create subcategories for each group. Here, it is useful to sort the items by color, size, shape, type, or any other criteria that you prefer.

Then, you can transfer the items into their proper storage. This is where you can use your containers, racks, and other organizers that you might have purchased. Although you might feel as though you know where each of the items is, it's good to still keep reminders by your side. For this, it's advisable to use labels or tags. This will help you keep track of what's in each container, bag, or box.

Making Decisions: Keep, Donate, Sell, or Throw Out?

How do you decide on what you want to keep, what you wish to donate or sell, or what would you rather throw out?

You can start by looking at whether the item is useful. If an item serves a purpose and you've used it recently, you should probably keep it. However, just because you may not be using a certain item doesn't mean that it needs to be thrown out. Likewise, if you use a tool or an item, but it is damaged or brings back hard feelings, then it can be replaced. For example, some of us stick with certain tools and supplies just because we're used to using them, even if the item is no longer working properly or we associate bad feelings with that item. There is a certain psychology around keeping items that have negative associations. Oftentimes, if we don't know how or we're not ready to process certain difficult feelings, we tend to keep reminders of it in our proximity. In fact, people might think that an item has positive associations for them. Only after revealing what looking at the item makes them feel, (e.g. guilt, shame, nervousness), do they realize that the background of the connection is actually negative. Their mindset can shift completely after a while, and they may start to resent a memory that they used to love because they've become aware of their true feelings.

The next thing that you want to check is whether the item is beautiful, or has any aesthetic appeal. This is important because, if the item is useful, you can keep it both as a utility and a decoration. In the realm of home organization, useful items that are decorative at the same time are extremely sought after. On the one hand, letting go of decorations that don't have useful value is a good way to minimize your household. However, taking that philosophy too far can lead to a home feeling cold and incomplete. If you want the bulk of your items to have useful value, but you want them to be decorative, then you should keep items that you don't use that much that simply look beautiful.

Finally, think about whether an item has sentimental value. Sentimental value of our items is really important, despite what people intent on ultimate minimalism might say. You might have positive, negative, or conflicting feelings toward your items. However, this shouldn't be the main criteria for whether or not you want to keep the items or let them go. This is because some of our memories and experiences may be important and feel like a part of our wholesome, lived-experienced, despite them being sad or unfortunate. Instead of asking yourself whether or not a certain item makes you happy, think about the meaning it has for you and whether or not you want to leave it as a legacy to your loved ones.

Think about whether you've used the item in the past year and if you're likely to use it again.

If the item has sentimental value, think about what's the best way to sort it and organize it. Review the memories associated with the item, and reflect on whether or not you should keep the item based on that.

Here are some of the best decision-making strategies for Swedish Death Cleaning:

- If there are too many items with sentimental value, or the item is significant but tricky to store in the long run, (e.g. children's drawings), **taking a photo** of it will preserve the positive memories associated with the item without making extra clutter.
- **Try the "one-year rule."** This rule helps you decide on the utility of an item, and it goes like this: if you haven't used an item, (a piece of clothing, a chair, etc.), during the past year, then you should consider donating or throwing it out.
- **Consider what your loved ones like and prefer.** When deciding on keeping or passing down items, keep your friends and family in mind. The importance of this is twofold: you don't want to leave them with an emotional burden of taking

things they don't like just to please you or honor your memory, and you also don't want to throw out items that they like or might find useful. Remember that knick-knacks that might be extra for you might be significant to other people, as the expense of decorating a home and purchasing small yet necessary tools and supplies, (e.g. glasses, office supplies, books, paintings, etc.), can amount to major costs. For example, whenever I wish to throw an item that's in decent shape, I take pictures of it and send them out in my friends and family chat groups. More often than not, there's at least one person who likes the item and would want to keep it.

Organizing Sentimental Belongings and Memorabilia

Why is organizing sentimental belongings and memorabilia so important? Organizing these items that have sentimental, decorative, antique, or collectible value can help preserve not only memories associated with those things, and make it easier to share the memories with your friends and family, but also increase the value of your legacy over items. Actually, it's hard to know if an item has antique value before an expert checks it out. Because of this, make sure to take pictures of your older items and send them to either the nearest local antique shop or an online service that specializes in antiques to find out.

Organizing and sorting items of non-utilitarian value can help reduce the work that your family needs to do after you pass away. You can help them by letting them know which of your items are important to you and why. Sometimes, loved ones keep items that they don't really need just because you've used them a lot, and that's a shame. For example, I had one really unflattering gray hoodie that I actually didn't like. The only good thing about it was that it was warm enough for me to snuggle during cold winter days, and I wore it all the time for a while. When my little daughter had a school assignment to write about her parents, she noted that my gray hoodie was one of my favorite things. She had seen me wear it all the time and had no idea how eager I was to get rid of it. I imagine that, had she formed an emotional association with me wearing that hoodie as one of her childhood memories, she might end up keeping that ugly thing that I was, in fact, eager to donate. Now, imagine how many of your items your loved ones might be associating with you, thinking that they are important, that you actually don't like that much and wouldn't want to be associated with them. This is why it's important for your family to know what is and what isn't important to you. Imagine the irony of keeping a dress or a suit that you actually can't stand, but were keeping as a memory of someone you love, only for your family to end up remembering you by it and carrying on the unfortunate tradition. Ouch.

How should you organize sentimental belongings and memorabilia?

Consider grouping your sentimental belongings by:

- Theme.
- Event (vacation, a beloved family member, or life milestone).
- Use labels to track each category or group.
- Go digital. Create a digital archive of important videos, photos or documents. You can also use cloud

memory to store the digital copies and share the account with friends and family. This will preserve them for future generations without creating extra clutter.

Managing Paperwork and Important Documents

Now, you might be thinking, why is it so important to manage all of your important documents and paperwork? Managing personal and estate paperwork, as well as your important documents can help get your affairs in order in time. This will make it easier for your family to take care of you when you start struggling with getting treatments, medical, and other assistance. It can also help them take care of your estate after you pass away with full insight into the things you own and their value.

Doing so can also help you stay organized and up-to-date with your current appointments and commitments, first and foremost. In fact, keeping paper clutter can make you feel like you have more things to get to than you actually have. It can also make you look over other important commitments, like doing repairs, inspections, and other things that help maintain your health and property. Similar goes for any banking-related issues. You might think that you owe a certain amount only to discover that your rates went significantly up or down over time, or that your savings have amounted to different figures than you anticipated. Pay attention to insurance policies as well, as the years go by. The policy makers might have made changes that you forgot about that affect your future decisions. Doing all of this can help ease stress and anxiety for both you and your family.

Although you might feel eager to downsize on your paperwork, there are some documents that are extremely important to keep. Some important documents to keep include: insurance policies, debt reports, account reports, credit card balance and checkbooks, medical documentation, estate documentation, wills, trusts, and powers of attorney. You should also keep several copies of important personal paperwork, like birth certificates, marriage certificates, and passports.

Now that you know which of your documents you should definitely be keeping, let's take a deeper look at how you should organize paperwork and important documents. Organizing paperwork and documents can be more fun than you think. Embrace color coding and cool-looking folders, and you'll find what you thought to be cumbersome work feel almost like an art project. But, before you do that, a small note on throwing out paperwork. First things first, you don't need to keep everything. You can check whether your bank account balance and reports contain records of payments that can still be claimed in case of a glitch in electronic payment systems, which sadly can happen. This is particularly important if you have loans, mortgages, or credit card debts that can potentially be claimed due to technicalities and system errors.

When it comes to organizing your paperwork, a logical and simple filing system is the way to go when it comes to tracking important documents. Applying labels and sticky notes will keep track of everything that is in the file. Personally, I prefer using sticky notes as you can easily remove them and change the writing as documents within a file or a folder change. Paperwork that's not essential to keep in a digital form can be turned into a digital archive. Doing so is important to ensure that all of your documents are secure and easily accessible.

Chapter 4: Practical Tips for Swedish Death Cleaning

Great work! You're almost half-way through your Swedish death cleaning manual. By now, you've learned how to sort, categorize, and clean various areas of your home as you go. However, it takes a bit more knowledge and skill to persist with the purging all the way through and create a more functional living space.

Tackling Different Areas of Your Home

One of the first practical tips for Swedish Death cleaning is to focus on a single area at a time. Gradual progress in this sense has several advantages over other potential strategies, like organizing all items at once by type, (e.g. paperwork, memorabilia, clothes and linens), in the entire home. These advantages are:

- **Gradual learning.** Starting small is the way to go when it comes to purging. It gives you enough time to figure out what your ideal pace to work at when it comes to pulling items out, sorting, and cleaning. Over time, you'll become faster and better at it.
- **Seeing the results right away.** The very first time I decided to try purging and organizing, and long before I learned about Swedish death cleaning,

I thought it was smart to "eat the frog" and do the most difficult items at once. For me, it was clothing at the laundry. Now, imagine how smart of me it was to pull out all fabric-like items at once. I emptied every closed, linen drawer, and laundry drawer in my home. Doing all that to begin with drained so much of my energy, and I barely did any real work. I ended up living in a mess for about a week, unable to purge, sort, and organize all of the clothing and linens at the pace in which I planned (it was ambitiously meant to be done in a single afternoon). I will never repeat that mistake again! Now, I tend to start from a single shelf, usually the one that bugs me the most. Once I have one of them figured out, I'm able to tell how much time it took, and calculate how long I'll need to do a whole closet based on that. Doing so makes me feel like I made instant progress, and prevents frustration and loss of motivation.

- **One-and-done benefit.** When you're organizing one area at a time, you can tick it off your list and know that you're done with it for the time being. You can completely let it go and focus all of your mental and physical energy on other areas. Leaving various areas of your home unfinished can cause you to jump from one area to another like a frightened bunny, slowly forgetting what was already done and what is yet to be done. This makes the work unnecessarily difficult and causes you to rush decisions when it comes to keeping or letting go of items. There are a couple of reasons why it is important to tackle different areas of your home.

Different areas of your home may be housing different types of things, or be in need of different strategies for purging and organizing. For example, a different approach is needed for your kitchen than it is for your home office. Likewise, you'll be using different organizers and cleaners. To tackle several areas at a time means to sign up for going back-and-forth between different cleaning and organizing strategies, which can be exhausting. Doing a single type of item, one area at a time, prevents this hassle.

In this sense, tackling various areas of your home that contain similar items can help you stay better organized and make visible progress toward your goals. For example, after you've spent a couple of hours organizing one closet, you'll have a lot easier time doing the same for a couple more closets. You'll already have learned the best folding and sorting strategies, and you've exercised them enough to move faster and with more precision. But, what areas of your home should you tackle first?

Knowing where to start is a great way for you to set yourself up for success and remove any sense of hardship and difficulty right in the beginning. First, think about organizing those areas that are causing you the most stress or anxiety. Those could be the areas that you weren't getting around to organizing for years, or areas that you most associate with difficult feelings. I remember avoiding organizing and purging my and my sister's children's room for months after I moved into our old house. Just the thought of disrupting the vibe of that room was too much for me to handle. It didn't stop me from using spaces under the bed and tops of the closets for storage though, which meant that, over time, the room had accumulated so many other things I was refusing to let go of. However, once I finally got around to organizing it, it turned out that the decisions about what to keep and what to let go of were fairly easy. My sister's old jewelry had almost entirely oxidized and rusted, so there was no other choice but to throw it out. Some of the items that I thought were terribly important were no more but reminiscent of our teen times. An adult me didn't seem to have much emotional attachment for those items at all. Or, you can simply start with areas that are most cluttered. This might sound scary, but don't worry. It is a justified thing to do as the said area is most likely having a negative effect on your life and health. If your library is the messiest area, for example, the dust and bacteria that it might be spreading could have direct connections with some of your allergies or sleep problems. If it is your study or home office, a messy household paperwork might be keeping you from addressing due issues, like permits, licenses, or inspections. You don't know until you look!

If you are like me, and you've started to enjoy purging and organizing a lot, you might see the messiest areas as both the most intense and the most interesting to work on. You want to "save the best for last," in which case, snowballing might be the best idea. This technique is also recommended to people whose health and strength limitations might keep them from giving the entire home due attention. In that case, you might want to start with areas that are easiest to declutter, such as a single drawer or closet. You will see gradual, notable progress. This will encourage you to keep going, and by the time you reach those most difficult areas, you will have gathered enough confidence and motivation to see the process through.

How to Approach Organizing Your Home by Areas

Now, let's talk about organizing in a bit more detail. Let's begin from everyone's favorite emotional rollercoaster— the bottom of a large, old closet. As you open it, you might start feeling like crying for more than one reason. It might be random items piled up one atop the other, spreading dust and making you cough and sneeze. You might be thinking about what all of those items mean to you, and start feeling a wave of sadness at the thought of all the people and memories of past times. The fact that you have a cloth and a cleaning spray in your hand are about to spend hours going through one item at a time doesn't make things better. It is difficult, for sure, and I fully empathize with you. But, if you now decide to leave the area for another time, you might not get to it at all. It's time to calm and collect yourself, and figure out what to do first one task at a time. To start with, think about breaking down the area into a series of smaller tasks. You could start from pulling items out, and cleaning each of them while doing so. As you do that, you can place each item in its designated organizer (storage box, folder, or bag). Right after you've done that, you should give the old closet a good cleaning, after which you can return the boxes that you decided to keep. Now that you have everything planned out, you can start tackling one task at a time. I learned after organizing several homes just how important it is to have the whole scenario planned out ahead of time. When you have an idea of what you're about to do clearly mapped out for yourself, the work starts to look a lot more manageable.

Next, map out your organizing approach using the most efficient sorting and categorizing strategies that you previously used for your goods and items, and make thought-through decisions about what to keep, donate, sell, or throw out. Changes are that you're not so bad at organizing, as most people aren't, as you are attached to items because you fear losing them. Most people, myself included, think along the lines of "I can always get rid of this if I choose to, but once I do it, it's too late to change my mind." This often leads us to keep items longer than we're supposed to simply because it's never the right time to address them. Now, it's time to move away from that feeling. You likely have an intuitive organizing approach that matches your personality and how you use your items. Where you place items on a shelf, (whether more to the left or to the right), and how you display the most significant ones, (whether at the center of a surface or more toward the wall, to protect them from harm), speaks a lot about your intuitive preference. Although you might find a lot of great organizing advice in the realm of interior design (e.g. occupy only 50% of the storage space, shuffle item size and color, etc.), none of the principles will feel comfortable if they don't match your personality. Now that you've purged and sorted your items, start by simply arranging them the way you like best. Only change that layout if there are functional obstacles (e.g. your door might hit the lamp or books are getting in the way of using an electric outlet) or if there are safety concerns (the item might fall down and break). Make adjustments slowly and when needed, all while thinking about whether or not you're comfortable with the arrangement.

Strategies for Downsizing and Decluttering

Now, let's talk a bit more about how to properly reduce the volume and number of your belongings. What are the right strategies to downsize and declutter your home? While there are several strategies to choose from, a couple of them pair with Swedish Death Cleaning better than most. Here are the steps for using those strategies:

- **Think about using the "one in, one out" rule.** This rule entails that you donate or throw out one item per each new item that you bring into your home. This principle affects your shopping choices as well, as you start to decide on what to let go of the moment you decide to buy a new thing. If there's nothing that you wish to get rid of for the sake of getting your new item, perhaps you don't need it. This principle also prevents re-cluttering your home after all of the work is done to purge.
- **Try out the "four-box method."** This method means that you sort all of your things into four large boxes: throw out, keep, donate, or sell. In my experience, deciding on what to throw out first is the best way to downsize, so I tend to fill that box first. Once I've decided that the remaining items

aren't in bad-enough shape to be thrown out, and now knowing just how few items there are to organize, I tend to proceed with a lot more energy, thought, and patience. If you decide what to throw out first, you won't feel pressure to keep as few items as possible. Instead, you'll make more authentic decisions.

- Finally, you can **think about hiring a professional organizer or a decluttering coach to help you out.** These experts know dozens of different organizing methods and principles, and they will also help you find an organizing layout that will work best for you, your home, and your family. They will tell you exactly which organizers to get, in which design, shape, and size. That way, you can focus on the intellectual and emotional work of deciding what to keep and what to let go of.

Efficient Storage Solutions

Finding the right storage solution is perhaps the most daunting task of all, especially if you're organizing for the first time. While you'll find a ton of seemingly beautiful and functional solutions online, they might not turn out to be so great in the long run. For example, they might change color over time (turn yellow or pale), or they might be difficult to clean. Despite them being "just" tools to organize your items, storage solutions can get quite expensive. In fact, it could take between several hundred to several thousands of dollars to get all the solutions that you need, and in the right color, size, and shape for your living space. It's better to "rip the bandaid" right away and tell you that you should think about getting organizing solutions as getting brand new pieces of furniture or decor. Because of this, before you start, map out a rough budget to use when making storage decisions. With that in mind, you can continue to reflect on other important issues.

Efficient storage solutions, like boxes, racks, hanging organizers, caskets, drawer dividers, and others, can help you keep your home organized in the long run. They can also help you make the most of your living space, and find functional use for all of the corners, countertops, and spaces under your furniture. That way, you can keep some of the non-essential items away, while freeing up more space. They can also make it easier to find and access the things you need.

But, what are some of the more efficient storage solutions?

- You can think about using storage containers, shelves, or hooks to help keep your goods and assets organized.
- Use labels or tags to help keep track of what's in each container or on each shelf.
- Think about using vertical space, such as wall-mounted shelves or hanging organizers.

Dealing With Digital Clutter

Digital clutter refers to the accumulation of digital files, such as emails, photos, and documents, that can clutter up your digital devices and make it difficult to find what you need. But, how to deal with digital clutter? Here are the basic steps:

- Start by organizing your digital files into folders or categories, and deleting any files you no longer need.
- Think about using cloud storage or an external hard drive to store important files and free up space on your devices.
- Use filters to automatically sort and organize your emails.
- Make sure to unsubscribe from any newsletters or mailing lists you no longer need.

Chapter 5: Emotional and Social Aspects of Swedish Death Cleaning

Communicating Your Intentions and Wishes

While the basic concept of Swedish Death Cleaning revolves around you and the things you want, your family and loved ones are also affected by the decisions you make in this regard. Ask yourself: Would you like your loved ones to get rid of their significant things without consulting you first? Oftentimes, things that might be mundane to us are important to the people we love. For example, you might have an old outfit that you don't particularly like, and you wouldn't mind donating it. But, your family associates that outfit with you and some happy times you had together. Maybe, they would want to keep those items. The same might go for your furniture or seemingly irrelevant knick knacks, like old combs, walking canes, or shaving equipment. For example, I treasure those exact items from my late parents dearly. I kept my grandfather's walking cane, his old-school razor, and my grandmother's old-fashioned comb for decades now. If I were to ask them, those items may not have been important to them at all, and they might even feel like it was about time to replace them. But, I have fond childhood memories of watching my grandfather walk slowly with his cane, and it was so incredibly interesting to watch him shave. My grandmother would take her time to fix her hair before she'd take me out to play, and I remember how I used to love watching her create beautiful hairstyles with that one single ebony comb. However, my grandparents were also attached to some other things that I barely knew of. Grandma had a valuable broach that she wanted me to keep, and grandpa cherished his old chess set. The set was hand-carved and purchased on one of their journeys, and my family might have sold it after their passing if we didn't know how important that set was for him. Why am I mentioning all this? other people may not have the same perception of which items are important to you and which aren't, just as you might not be fully aware of which of your items are important to them.

Beyond making sure that you and your loved ones are on the same page regarding what's to be kept and what's to be donated or thrown out, you might need help from your family with the cleaning itself. Now, while Swedish death cleaning might be common in its homeland, mentioning it to your family, who might not be fully on board or familiar with the concept, might feel a bit sudden and overwhelming. They might not be ready or willing to "go there," or struggle and find it too sad to think about the future life that won't include you.

This is why it's so important for you to clearly state your intentions, goals and wishes in this regard. This can help your friends and family better understand what your goals are with Swedish Death Cleaning. If you remember from the earlier chapters, there might be several different goals with this type of purging. The process of cleaning itself is thus more different. For example, if your primary goal is to get rid of extra items and enjoy a nicer layout in your home, it will be a whole different journey than if you are focusing on your legacy and making sure that your family knows who should keep which item after you pass away.

Communicating your goals ahead of time can also help prevent any potential misunderstandings or conflicts after you pass away. Your family members might want some of your items, and struggle to figure out who should keep what. Also, if they don't know what's important for you to keep and what's not, they might feel guilty and keep all of your belongings, out of which many or the majority might not be that important to you.

To sum up, share your intentions and observations regarding the value that your items have ahead of time to make sure that your family is well aware of them. This is also a great opportunity for you and your whole family to agree on the so-called 'family heirlooms' or items that shouldn't be passed down to a single person. Instead, they belong to the family as a whole, and they should be kept in a more neutral place where everyone can access them when needed, and then take them back once they no longer need them (e.g. antiques, valuable cutlery or linens, family jewels, etc.). If there's currently no place where these items can be safely kept so that everyone has equal access, then perhaps you should consider storing them in a bank vault and including them in your will. That way, you ensure that everyone's rights and responsibilities are assigned accordingly, and more importantly, that the agreement will be kept.

The Best Way to Communicate Your Intentions and Wishes

When it comes to confronting the idea of leaving your items as a legacy, it's best to be honest and open with your loved ones. Start with a conversation in which both you and your friends and family will express observations and opinions. This conversation should come after you've written out a purging plan for yourself, and clearly outlined which items have a place in your home and as your legacy, and which ones are up to your family to decide what to do with. In that regard, leaving it to your family to decide what to do with the items you're letting go of is both kind and useful to take some work off of your shoulders. If there are items that your friends and family would like to take right away that you no longer want in your home, they can come and pick them up before you even start sorting and organizing.

But, sometimes a conversation alone isn't enough to specify your legacy ideas. If there are a lot of items to distribute, or you're not sure if the agreement that you had with your family will hold, you should consider writing a letter or creating a video message. You can share it with your friends and family, so there's a permanent trace of your wishes. This is also a great solution if having a live conversation is too difficult for you and your family members.

If you're talking to your family and friends directly, be clear and specific. Make sure to clearly state how many items you wish to pass on, which are significant to you and why, and what you wish to be done with those items after your passing. After clearing out what your wishes, consider your friend's and family's feedback and questions.

Handling Family Heritage and Inherited Things

Some of your items might not belong entirely to you. They might be from your deceased relatives, or they might belong to your spouse's family. That changes the perspective regarding what should be done with those items and memorabilia. Before I move on to clarify this a bit further, I would advise getting legal assistance and consulting an attorney regarding what's the best way to tackle family heritage. Although various family members might have emotional attachments to some memorabilia or assets, or feel like they earned them more than others, there actually might be some legal requirements that apply when it comes to heritage. Make sure to go over this topic with some hired counsel so that you avoid potential discomfort or emotional hurt for your family in case the heritage ends up being handled differently than you agreed on.

Family heritage may have sentimental or historical value. It also might have antique value, which further adds to its economic value and affects how the items should be preserved, passed down, and treated. In that sense, these items might be more important to your family's legacy than you anticipated. In that sense, handling the items carefully can help make sure that they're preserved for future generations. So, what's the best way to handle family heritage while honoring everyone's wishes?

First, think about including your family members in the entire decision-making process. After writing down a list of the heirlooms and other items of emotional and other value, hear out your family and their opinions. This is a great opportunity to get a clearer idea about how the items should be handled, which memories your family associates with the said heritage, and what they would want to be done with it.

In the spirit of this book, pay close attention to properly preserving family heirlooms. This is the matter of proper storage and care, first and foremost. Unlike your regular items that are likely suitable for regular storage on shelves and in closets, more valuable items might need extra protection. Depending on the material, they might need to be stored in air-tight containers, laminated, or protected with different chemicals to prevent damage due to air exposure, temperature changes, humidity, and light. Paintings, for example, as well as photographs, are quite sensitive to light. Their color might fade out over time, which can be prevented with proper preservation methods. Porcelain and metal objects can rust and oxidize, while jewels can get scratched or broken. As you can see, sorting them all neatly in a storage box, in this case, may not suffice.

Navigating Sensitive Conversations

Now, you might be wondering, why are you reading about how to talk to your family in a book about cleaning and organizing? Well, Swedish death cleaning is a wholesome process that is done inside-out. First, you come to terms with keeping or letting go of items on your own, and the second part of this transformative process is to process all of the complex feelings and opinions with your family. While the idea of having that kind of a sensitive conversation with your friends and family is scary, rest assured that it will have a comforting impact later on. Your family will be certain in your wishes and won't have any doubt about what to do with your belongings.

Sensitive conversations are important because they ensure that everyone is on the same page. They prevent misunderstandings and conflicts after you pass away, and allow your family to grieve in a healthier way, by leaning into one another for support in coping and celebrating your life. Having tension and conflict regarding heritage is the last thing you want for your loved ones, isn't it?

Having an open conversation with your friends and family members can help prevent, address, and ease any concerns or issues that may arise during the cleaning process. For example, if your family members that are helping out with cleaning find out for the first time that you plan to donate or throw out some things they love, they might feel really hurt. Or, if you intend to pass down an item to a family member, and another family member wants it dearly, tensions might arise. It's hard to tell what's worse though, whether the conflict erupts while you're having all of your possessions taken out to be organized, or when you're no longer around to help resolve it.

Navigating sensitive conversations, in this regard, should be handled gently and gracefully. First, start from having your own, clear plan for your belongings. But, also understand that there will be as many different perspectives and opinions as there are close friends and family members. Some of their opinions might not fully align with yours, which makes it that more important to compromise. Here, to compromise means to be willing to look at your belongings from the perspective of your loved ones. For example, it could be very important for you that your oldest living relative inherits a certain item. However, they might not be very interested in it, or may not have the time, means, or possibility to take care of it properly. On the other hand, there might be a family member who values the said item a lot more. They might be willing to take care of it properly and they might value it as much as you do, or even more. In this case, it would be wise to adapt your wishes to what's best for everyone. There is one particularly sad scenario though, and it is when items are valuable to us, but our family members don't have the same attachment to them or may not want to take good care of them. It might be a hard pill to swallow, however, try putting yourself in their shoes. What if someone came to you with an item that you didn't like, and wanted you to take care of it for life? What if the item that you don't like begins with required maintenance, or a lot of regular care? In that case, it would be fair to pass down an item to a person who will appreciate it more.

Having difficult conversations in which you'll voice your desire to move forward with Swedish death cleaning may not be easy for you and your family. However, it is vital for everyone to get on the same page and for everyone's opinions to be properly heard and understood.

Chapter 6: Workbook—Exercises and Activities

Reflecting on Your Belongings and Their Significance

I recommend reevaluating things that you consider valuable, as it can help you understand why they matter to you. This can make it easier for you to decide what to keep, store, display, donate, or throw out. To reflect on your belongings and their significance, I advise that you take some time to look over the trickiest items and consider their history and importance. It would be helpful to also write down your thoughts and feelings about items you're struggling to decide on. Then, you can share the reflections with friends and family. You could even create a scrapbook or memory box to keep the memories associated with your items. Here are some useful reflective questions in thaT regard:

What does your relationship with your belongings look like right now?

Example

Do you have trouble letting go of things, even if you don't use them? Do you feel overwhelmed by the amount of things you have? Do you feel like your things are taking over your living space?

Reflecting on your belongings and their significance can be a challenging but rewarding process. Here are some questions and a questionnaire to help you get started:

- What's your relationship with your things like right now?
- Do you have trouble letting go of things, even if you don't use them?
- Do you feel overwhelmed by the amount of things you have?
- Do you feel like your things are taking over your living space?

Questionnaire:

- List all of your possessions for a single room (bedroom, living room, or pantry), categorized into:
  - "keep,"
  - "donate/sell," and
  - "throw away."
- Example: Items to categorize:
  - Clothes you haven't worn in over a year,
  - books you've already read and don't plan on reading again,
  - kitchen appliances, utensils, and gadgets you never use.

Writing Your Personal Stories and Memories

Writing your personal stories and memories can help you preserve personal and family legacy and ensure that family history and heritage are passed down to future generations. It can also be a great way to reflect on your life and the experiences that shaped you. To write your personal stories and memories, start by:

- Brainstorming a list of significant events or experiences in your life,
- Writing down your memories and reflections about each important item, and
- Think about organizing them into a theme or a timeline.
- Sharing your stories with friends and family, or
- Publish them in a memoir or other written work.

Here are some reflective questions to consider when writing your personal stories and memories:

- What are some of your significant memories associated with said belongings?
- How are these belongings associated with your growth as a person?
- What are some of the most important lessons that you associate with the items?
- What are some of the most important relationships associated with the items, and how have they affected you?

You can use either a computer, tablet, or a regular notebook or journal for this task. Whichever method you choose, make sure that it works for you and that you feel relaxed and comfortable.

Designing Your Ideal Living Space

Designing your ideal living space can help you shape a home that will truly reflect your personality and values, as well as support your physical and mental well-being. It can also be a way to create a sense of ease and security. To organize your ideal living space, first pinpoint what your priorities and preferences are. For example, you could like a certain interior style, a more open space, or specific colors or textures. Consider working with a skilled designer or interior decorator to help you create a wholesome and functional space. Be open to experimentation and change, and willing to adjust your home layout as your needs and preferences change over time.

Here are some tips and ideas to help you design your ideal living space:

- Use color and texture to create a mood or atmosphere in your home.
- Consider using natural materials, such as wood or stone, to create a sense of warmth and comfort.
- Use lighting to create a sense of depth and dimension in your space.
- Consider using plants or other natural elements to bring life and energy into your home.
- Use furniture and accessories to create a sense of balance and harmony in your space.

Creating a Legacy Plan

Creating a legacy plan can help make sure that your wishes are honored after you pass away. It can also ensure that your personal and financial affairs are in order, and that your personal and family legacy lives on. Your legacy plan should include a will, a trust, and other relevant documents that attest to and guarantee honoring of your wishes for how your assets should be handled after your passing. It should also include instructions for how any dependents or pets should be taken care of, as well as a plan for how your family heritage should be maintained, kept, used, and distributed. Consider including a clear statement of your personal values and beliefs , so that your family and friends better understand your wishes and decisions.

Here are some reflective questions to consider when creating your legacy plan:

- What are your highest personal values and beliefs?
- What do you want your ultimate legacy to be?
- Who do you want to pass down your assets and possessions after your passing?
- How do you want your dependents or pets to be cared for, and who is the best person to do that?

Your Swedish Death Cleaning Plan

Create a checklist of items you need to start your Swedish Death Cleaning journey.

Example:

Items:

- Large trash bags or boxes for items to throw away,
- boxes and bags for items to donate/sell,
- cleaning supplies for deep cleaning your living space,
- labels and a label maker, a clipboard and a notepad, and writing supplies.

Consider creating a timeline for your Swedish Death Cleaning journey, like:

- Day 1–5: Decluttering and organizing the bedroom.
- Day 6–10: Decluttering and organizing your kitchen.
- Day 11–15: Decluttering and organizing your living room.
- Day 16–20: Deep cleaning your entire living space.

Practical Examples:

Here are some practical examples that you can take to create a personal development plan for your Swedish Death Cleaning:

Identify Personal Long-Term Goals

1.Declutter and organize living space over the next year and/or create a more minimalist lifestyle.

2. Create a legacy plan for your belongings and set your personal and financial matters in order.

3. Downsize your living space and move into a smaller house or apartment.

Break down long-term goals into more manageable steps:

Practical Examples:

1. Decluttering and organizing:

- Start by decluttering one room at a time,
- create a system for organizing your belongings, and
- maintain a regular cleaning schedule.

2. Creating a legacy plan:

- Research different estate planning options,
- consult with an attorney or financial planner, and
- discuss your wishes with loved ones.

3. Downsizing and moving:

- Research different living options,
- create a budget for moving expenses, and
- start decluttering and organizing your belongings ahead of time.

Set Realistic Goals
Practical Examples:

1. Be specific: Declutter and organize my bedroom this month.

2. Make them quantifiable: Create my legacy plan and run it by an attorney within the next three months.

3. Manageable: Downsize my living space and move into a smaller house no later than the end of the next year.

4. Meaningful: Use a personal value statement to set goals and communicate wishes to friends and family.

5. Timely: Declutter and organize my living space by the end of this year.

Embrace Feedback and Support From Loved Ones Practical Examples:

1. I should seek advice from a professional organizer or decluttering expert.

2. I need to discuss my legacy plan with loved ones and seek their input and feedback.

3. I must consult with a real estate agent or relocation specialist for advice on downsizing and moving.

4. I should be willing to adapt my plan as my needs and circumstances change. For example, I can:

- adjust my decluttering and organizing plan as I encounter unexpected challenges or obstacles,
- update my legacy plan as my personal or financial circumstances change,
- be open to changing my living space or downsizing plan if my needs or preferences change over time.

Here are some reflective questions to consider when writing your personal statement and Swedish death cleaning plan:

What Are Your Long-Term Goals and Aspirations?
Practical Examples:

1. To declutter and organize my living space by the end of the next year, start living a more minimalist lifestyle.

2. To create my personal family legacy plan and set my affairs in order.

3. To downsize my living space and move into a smaller, more manageable living space.

What Are Your Strengths and Weaknesses?
Practical Examples:

1. I am good at letting go of sentimental items, but I struggle with letting go of items that have a monetary value.

2. I am organized and efficient, but I have a hard time with deep cleaning and maintaining a clean living space.

3. I am resourceful and creative, but I find it difficult to make decisions about what to keep and what to let go of.

What Are Some Areas for Growth and Improvement?
Practical Examples:

1. I should research the value of items and sell them online or at a consignment shop, seek advice from an appraiser or antiques dealer, and donate items that are not valuable when letting go of items with monetary value.

2. I should create a cleaning schedule and stick to it, declutter regularly to prevent buildup, and seek advice

from a professional cleaner or organizer to deep clean and maintain a clean living space.

3. I should use a checklist or criteria to help make decisions, seek advice from friends or family, and practice mindfulness and self-reflection to identify what items truly bring joy and value to my life when making decisions about what to keep and what to let go of.

What Resources and Support Do You Have for Achieving Your Goals?
Practical Examples:

To declutter and organize, I will:

- use a decluttering guide or workbook,
- Get advice from a professional organizer, and
- enlist the help of friends or family.

To create a legacy plan, I will:

- consult with an estate planning attorney,
- seek advice from a financial planner or accountant, and
- discuss my wishes with loved ones.

If I need to downsize and move, I will:

- research different living options,
- seek advice from a real estate agent or relocation specialist, and
- enlist the help of a moving company or professional organizer.

I can also consider using a personal development plan template or worksheet to help me organize my thoughts and create a roadmap for achieving my goals.

Practicing Mindfulness and Self-Care

I found that mindfulness and self-care helped me reduce a lot of stress, improve your emotional and physical health, and improve my well-being before I began with Swedish death cleaning. Mindfulness helped me be more present in the moment and pay attention to my own thoughts, feelings, and the environment without negative judgment. In this sense, self-care ensures that I am taking good care of my physical, emotional, and mental health. Because of this, I advise trying mindfulness and self-care, as well as incorporating activities like meditation, yoga, fitness, journaling, or spending time in nature into your daily routines. Treat yourself kindly, and prioritize your own physical and mental well-being.

Here are some tips and ideas to help you practice mindfulness and self-care:

Practicing Mindfulness
Practical Examples:

1. Take a few minutes each day to sit quietly and focus on your breath.

2. Practice mindful decluttering by being present at the moment and paying attention to your thoughts and feelings as you let go of items.

3. Use a mindfulness app or guided meditation to help you stay focused and present.

Practicing Self-Care
Practical Examples:

1. Take breaks throughout the day to stretch or move your body, especially if you are spending a lot of time decluttering or organizing.

2. Prioritize sleep and make sure you are getting enough rest each night to help you feel refreshed and energized.

3. Practice self-compassion by being kind to yourself and acknowledging your accomplishments, no matter how small.

Incorporating Activities Into Your Daily Routine
Practical Examples:

1. Practice yoga or stretching exercises to help you stay relaxed and flexible.

2. Spend time in nature by taking a walk or sitting outside to help reduce stress and improve your mood.

3. Write in a journal to help you process your thoughts and feelings about the decluttering process.

Practicing Gratitude
Practical Examples:

1. Write down things you are thankful for each day, such as the progress you've made in decluttering or the support of loved ones.

2. Take time to appreciate the items you are keeping and the memories they hold.

3. Practice gratitude by expressing your appreciation to loved ones who have helped you with the Swedish Death Cleaning process.

Prioritizing Your Well-Being
Practical Examples:

1. Take breaks when you need them and don't push yourself too hard.

2. Seek support from friends or family if you are feeling overwhelmed or stressed.

3. Practice self-care regularly to help you stay focused and energized throughout the decluttering process.

Chapter 7: Maintaining an Organized Life

Now that you've successfully gone through the entire process of Swedish death cleaning, it's time for you to figure out a plan to stay organized in the long run. Remember, you don't need to settle for organizing just once! You can declutter, organize, reorganize, and purge your possessions as many times as you want or need. With that in mind, it would be good if you had a strategy to avoid the build-up of clutter so that each time you organize and purge is easier. In fact, despite learning so much about organizing, it's likely that you won't be able to stay perfectly organized all the time. Yet, some of the most important things have been done. You've learned how to keep a detailed list of your belongings, and how to handle more meaningful and valuable items. You now know that you need to store them in a way that's most suitable to keep them safe and undamaged. This is important to keep in mind, as some of your belongings that are important to your loved ones may be relatively new, and not require any particular storage. You also might get more valuables in the years to come, so the list of important items will get larger. Now, it's time to figure out the smartest and most practical steps for you to take in the long run to stay as organized as you are now. Here's where to start.

Creating Sustainable Habits and Routines

Now that you've had an opportunity to evaluate all of your items, you probably noticed that some of your habits might be causing clutter. For example, you might not immediately get rid of shopping bags, wrapping paper, or receipts that you paid for, and you end up storing them in a corner or the bottom of a drawer. Or, you might pile up clothing without thinking about which items you wear and which ones you don't. In fact, guilt over getting rid of functioning items that we simply don't need is a major reason why so many people pile up items and choose against letting go. It goes for makeup and cosmetics that you're not using, clothes, as well as furniture and dishes. However, in the long run, it is much kinder to give an item to someone than let it sit in your home until it is no longer usable. Aside from making sure to be more mindful of items that you're keeping in your home, another important step is to create more sustainable routines and habits.

Doing so helps you maintain a clutter-free and organized home in the long run. Regular decluttering routines prevent accumulating unnecessary items in the future and make all your further cleaning and organizing efforts easier. Having these routines is also a great way for you to reduce stress. Not only will your living space look better, but you'll also have an easier time keeping it clean and tidy. This can help you further increase productivity. In fact, clutter is known to be distracting and creates a sense of nervousness for anyone who is trying to focus on productive work. By eliminating clutter, you will feel a lot better in your space, and there will be nothing to distract you from your activities. With this in mind, here are some sustainable habits and routines that you can adopt to stay consistently organized:

- Tidy up and organize each day. Have a morning, midday, and evening routine for picking up and organizing items. Walk through each room and pick up items that don't belong there. Then, take them to their rightful 'home.'
- Throw it out like it's no joke. Remind yourself to throw out unnecessary items each time you come back home from shopping. This includes receipts, bags, broken items, and items that can be donated. To make this easier, keep a trash bin and a donation box in each of your rooms that tends to pile up clutter. That way, you'll simply throw out and designate items for donating, without delaying this decision and creating clutter in your home.
- Set aside regular time each week for decluttering and organizing. No matter how hard you try, chances are that you'll need to reorganize your home from time to time. Even if you don't have a build-up of clutter anytime, your needs and preferences when it comes to keeping and storing your items might change. With this, you might want a different layout and organizing system. You might also reveal that, over time, some of your organizing systems aren't as practical as you thought they would be. It is perfectly fine to make adjustments on

the go and reflect on your home organization on a weekly basis.

- Use the "one in, one out." As explained earlier in the book, this book means that you make a commitment to throw out one item per each item you buy. This rule may require a lot of discipline, but it will help you maintain an optimum number of belongings in the long run.
- Adopt your form of a minimalist lifestyle. While you may find different interpretations of minimalism, it essentially boils down to choosing to keep only the most valuable and meaningful items in your home. The upside to minimalism is that you can minimize your belongings so significantly as to start seeing drastic changes when it comes to keeping your home clean and decluttered. The downside of it though is that many people who tried, and eventually gave up minimalism claim that it eventually began causing them anxiety. They went to the extreme of being afraid of having too many items and fearing that they're wasting money if they spend on something non-essential. As a result, their quality of life began declining, and they eventually decided to drop the concept overall. With this in mind, you can consider finding your own balance when it comes to how many items you choose to keep. In my experience, a healthy dose of minimalism means having a mindful relationship with your possessions and buying things that make sense for you. This alone may eliminate many purchases that might be spontaneous and made out

of fear of missing out, especially when it comes to using sales and discounts.

Regular Maintenance and Re-Evaluation

Upon finishing your first Swedish death cleaning session, I recommend taking a step back and reevaluating your entire experience. I also recommend taking notes and observations, including how the process felt, the lessons you learned, and reminders for yourself about how you can make this process easier and better in the future. With this in mind, here are a couple more useful tips for maintaining your organized home and reevaluating your needs:

- Reflect on how you change. As time goes by, you are growing as a person, and your needs are changing as well. I remember, as a young, single woman, I wanted to live in a modern, spacious, yet minimalist home with as few belongings as possible. Later in life, as a mother to young children, I began yearning for a warmer interior and an abundance of belongings. Now that I aimed to shop weekly or monthly, I needed the space and organizing systems to house a large number of items. My interior style changed as well, and I started loving colors, layered textures, and children's art as well. All of this meant that my organizing layout changed. I made several transformations over the years, and I don't regret a single one.
- Ditch systems that don't work. If you notice that the way you organized some of your areas isn't working for you-change it. Let me give you another personal

example of how I started enjoying my clothes way more once I ditched a super-style, color-coordinated organization method. I noticed that I struggled to figure out outfits based on type and color coordination alone. My style preferences, instead, depended a lot more on my mood and how I saw my clothing items working together. Because of this, I simply switched to sorting items by how I liked to combine them. This helped me maintain a very neatly organized closet, as I instinctively knew where to hang a blouse or a pair of pants, as it was next to the items I was usually combining them with. You too are entitled to sorting your items in a way that works best for you, without feeling compelled to do it strictly by type, color, or size. Some people, for example, sort items by the order in which they use them. That way, they have the most essential items close by when needed, while the less frequently used items are tucked away in less visible storage spaces.

Incorporating Swedish Death Cleaning Principles Into Everyday Life

As you learned in this book so far, Swedish death cleaning has a couple of important principles that you can include in your daily life moving forward. This includes:

- Being gentle and kind. Swedish death cleaning is all about respecting yourself and your family legacy, and appreciating positive memories. These things, however, are highly individual. Your loved ones had a different perspective of you and your life, so they might like or dislike certain items based on that. Likewise, you have your own, deeply intimate memories and associations with certain items that you've gathered throughout life. It's important to remember that you are allowed to, and should allow yourself, to keep items that are dear to you hard. If an item makes you happy and it's meaningful, it doesn't have to be in good shape, pretty, or useful. It can be as old as ragged as can be, but you should honor yourself by keeping it. The same goes for understanding how your friends and family members feel. Even if you strongly dislike an item and you think it's completely useless, it might be very dear to them. In that case, honor your loved ones by finding a compromise and storing the items in question in a mutually agreeable way.

- Focusing on intrinsic value. Unlike other organizing methods, Swedish death cleaning focuses a great deal on what your important items mean for you and your family. In that sense, you should focus on being aware and appreciating that value each day. Whether you're shopping or deciding for or against keeping an item, think about what it means to you. This will help you make a lot more mindful decisions and avoid keeping items either out of fear of letting go, guilt, or thinking that you need them simply because everyone else is using them.
- Cherishing your memories and legacy. Downsizing and decluttering isn't about giving out items that you love. Instead, it's about clearing out those items that aren't meaningful or don't serve a purpose in your life, as well as identifying those items that have a special significance. These items should then be either proudly displayed so that you can enjoy them

each day, or carefully stored to be protected from damage or loss.

- Including your loved ones. In this sense, Swedish death cleaning beats many other organizing methods that strictly refer to the person who is choosing to organize. But, what if you're not living alone? What if people who you live with aren't as equally passionate about organizing as you are, or don't have the same priorities? In that case, compromise is needed, and you might benefit from including the other person in the decision-making process as well. Your friends and family should also be included when it comes to deciding what will be passed down and how, what will be donated, and what will be thrown out. While you alone have the right to decide against keeping items that you don't want, you should have open and honest conversations with your loved ones when it comes to handing down things. I advise giving them the option to take items that you don't need, and including them into any family heritage decisions that you might be making.

Sharing the Benefits With Others

If you're the first one in your closest environment to try Swedish Death Cleaning, your friends and family might be taken aback at first. They might even protest what you're doing, but it's important not to give up and stay consistent. Let your friends and family know how your life has changed for the better, and share your journey on your social media channels. You can take before and after pictures, and write notes about how differently you feel now that you have some major points resolved, like your family heritage. This will help your loved ones better understand the process and further support you in your efforts to stay organized.

Great work! You succeeded with your Swedish death cleaning. Now, all that is left for you to do is make a commitment to focus on the meaning and significance of your items and continue doing the best you can to stay organized in the future.

Conclusion

Great work! It may not have been easy, but you've persisted in your efforts with Swedish death cleaning. First and foremost, you learned that this form of purging and decluttering isn't as grim as you might think. Swedish death cleaning originated out of people's efforts to first make their own lives easier by letting go of items that they no longer need, and then help their loved ones have a clear idea about what to do with their belongings after they're gone. This form of purging and decluttering is more about being mindful and coming to terms with how you truly feel about your items, and then making important decisions about how you'll pass down those items. In *Master the Art of Swedish Death Cleaning [Döstädning]: A Charming, Practical, and Unsentimental Approach to Organize and Declutter Your Home and Life—Workbook Included*, you also learned:

1. The Basics of Swedish Death Cleaning

In this book, you learned that sorting and categorizing your possessions should be more about making important decisions. In a nutshell, you are to decide whether to keep, donate, sell, or throw out your items. Although this may sound like a lot of work, it can be significantly cut down if you talk to your family first and see if one or more people would like to take some of the items that you no longer need.

Next, you learned how important organizing sentimental items and memorabilia is for you and your family. Items that are important to you, whether or not they have historic or antique value, are worth attention and keeping. If you feel like an item is emotionally important to you, you can do your best and not save effort or resources in making sure that your memorabilia is protected from loss and destruction. However, you also learned that it's ok to let go of items that you once thought were important to you, but your memories, experiences, and feelings that you associate with said objects have changed. In that case, feel free to get rid or or pass the item down.

After that, you gained deeper insight into how you can better sort, categorize, and organize your paperwork. Remember, there are certain pieces of documentation that you should keep, even if you feel like you don't need them. This includes personal documentation, documentation related to your goods and assets, as well as your will. This might not be all of the paperwork that you should keep, so make sure to check with your attorney first.

2. Tackling Different Areas of Your Home

Organizing one area at a time is one of the most efficient strategies for downsizing and decluttering your home. If you take up too much work at once, you might run out of physical strength, patience, persistence, and inspiration to see the process through. To avoid this, it's important to plan out your decluttering process thoroughly and review potential limitations and obstacles that might occur along the way. As important it is to be methodical, it is important to use efficient storage solutions. Quality boxes, containers, racks, and space dividers might be a significant investment, but they will make your space a lot easier to manage and a lot more pleasant to be in. As it is important to purge physical objects, you should also deal with digital clutter. Address your subscriptions, email, and saved files to check if there are things that you could unsubscribe from or delete from your storage. This will help you have fewer disruptions during the day and be calmer and more productive, and it might also amount to significant savings once you give up on services that you're no longer using.

3. Communicating Your Intentions and Wishes

Communicating what you want to be done with your items is extremely important with Swedish death cleaning. Not only that this form of cleaning might be entirely new to your friends and family, but they also might worry that you will throw out some items that are dear and important to them. Remember, your idea about what's significant might be different from those of your loved ones. This is why it's so important to have a conversation with your loved ones, no matter how hard it might be, and be open and honest regarding what you want to do with your belongings. Likewise, you should listen to the feedback coming from your family. People who've known you for a long time might have some feedback to share. They might have an opinion about which household organizing layout might be better for you, and their opinions are worth hearing out. They also might have opinions regarding the items that you want to pass down. In that sense, addressing the cleaning process with your family ahead of time helps prevent potential conflict or tension to your loved ones.

4. Reflecting on Your Belongings and Their Significance

Perhaps the most important aspect of Swedish death cleaning is that you get to reminisce on the significance of each of your items. Some items might be extra, so you may decide to throw them out, while others might revive very important and positive memories. You may decide to keep those items, in which case you need suitable containers and storage solutions that will ensure that your most cherished items are safe. Other than that, efficient storage solution systems also help maximize your space, meaning that you can boost a lot of storage space, like under your bed and above closets, and then further use it to store items. You also learned how to successfully go through the entire process. First, start with timely preparation, and get all of your storage and cleaning supplies. Make sure that you're well rested and fed, because cleaning and organizing can be very exhausting. If possible, have a family member with you to help you out. Then, move through one area of your home at a time. As you slowly pull out your items, take a look at each and think about what's their significance to you and your life. Slow down, be gentle, and don't rush the process. Take your time to think about every item. Long-term, this can help you feel a lot better emotionally, and revive some of the seemingly forgotten memories.

5. Incorporating Swedish Death Cleaning Principles Into Everyday Life

After you gave your entire home thorough cleaning, sorting, and organizing, your next goal will be to stay organized long term. For this, try using strategies like keeping bins and boxes across your entire home, so that you can quickly and easily decide if you want to throw out or donate the items that you don't need. Other than that, you can commit to giving up one of your items if you purchase one. This prevents clutter from building up, and it also helps you make better shopping decisions.

Overall, trying out Swedish Death Cleaning and making an effort to purge your home can help you stay organized, reduce stress and clutter. Plus, with your personal and financial affairs in order, you can enjoy spending time with your loved ones without fearing that a conflict might erupt once you pass away. It can also be a way to connect with your past and your personal history, and preserve your legacy for future generations.

References

Magnusson, M. (2018). *The gentle art of Swedish death cleaning: How to free yourself and your family from a lifetime of clutter*. Simon and Schuster.

Manke, B., & Franziska Gollnhofer, J. (2020). *Freed From Desire–Consumers' Escape From Market Ideologies Through Decluttering Practices?*. ACR North American Advances.

Ouellette, L. (2019). Spark joy? Compulsory happiness and the feminist politics of decluttering. *Culture Unbound*, 11(3-4), 534-550.

Roster, C. A., & Ferrari, J. R. (2023). Having less: A personal project taxonomy of consumers' decluttering orientations, motives and emotions. *Journal of Consumer Affairs*, 57(1), 264-295.

https://unsplash.com/it/foto/x5-tEdHLqR0

https://unsplash.com/it/foto/CCJGadKQXxI

https://unsplash.com/it/foto/1dJfljc2tBk

https://unsplash.com/it/foto/n9Z5BdAY_vQ

https://unsplash.com/it/foto/fqIhGwELYPs

https://unsplash.com/it/foto/spAkZnUleVw

https://unsplash.com/it/foto/hU6L_FxdNC8

https://unsplash.com/it/foto/tszceVXBP0s

https://unsplash.com/it/foto/cqgnUEOaW0o

https://unsplash.com/it/foto/0Qf8ej5cXLc

https://unsplash.com/it/foto/ErOdIrDA6b0

https://unsplash.com/it/foto/h0j-H2jyFj4

https://unsplash.com/it/foto/ojZ4wJNUM5w

https://unsplash.com/it/foto/ngLt4Y1vI_Q

Made in United States
Troutdale, OR
09/08/2023

12746242R10056